MW01265567

SURVIVING AND THRIVING AT SCHOOL

By Shannon Berg

CONTENT CONSULTANT

Dr. Amy Bellmore
Professor of Human Development
University of Wisconsin–Madison

Essential Library

An Imprint of Abdo Publishing | abdobooks.com

abdobooks.com

Published by Abdo Publishing, a division of ABDO, PO Box 398166, Minneapolis, Minnesota 55439. Copyright © 2021 by Abdo Consulting Group, Inc. International copyrights reserved in all countries. No part of this book may be reproduced in any form without written permission from the publisher. Essential Library™ is a trademark and logo of Abdo Publishing.

Printed in the United States of America, North Mankato, Minnesota.
082020
012021

Cover Photo: Monkey Business Images/Shutterstock Images
Interior Photos: Seongjae Kim/iStockphoto, 8; Leo Patrizi/iStockphoto, 11; Andrija Nikolic/iStockphoto, 13; iStockphoto, 14, 16–17, 27, 35, 49, 62–63, 68, 70, 72, 76, 85, 94, 96; People Images/iStockphoto, 20; Africa Studio/Shutterstock Images, 22; Wave Break Media/Shutterstock Images, 24–25, 50–51; Light Field Studios/iStockphoto, 28; Monkey Business Images/iStockphoto, 32, 59; Media Photos/iStockphoto, 38; SDI Productions/iStockphoto, 40–41, 61, 64–65; Roberto Galan/Shutterstock Images, 44; Aleksandar Nakic/iStockphoto, 46–47; Monkey Business Images/Shutterstock Images, 52–53; Vitchanan Photography/Shutterstock Images, 56; Antonio Guillem/iStockphoto, 75; Vadym Petrochenko/iStockphoto, 80; G Point Studio/iStockphoto, 82; Stígur Már Karlsson/Heimsmyndir/iStockphoto, 86; Frame Stock Footages/Shutterstock Images, 88–89; DGL Images/iStockphoto, 92; Antonio Diaz/Shutterstock Images, 98

Editor: Aubrey Zalewski
Series Designer: Nikki Nordby

Library of Congress Control Number: 2019954325
Publisher's Cataloging-in-Publication Data

Names: Berg, Shannon, author.
Title: Surviving and thriving at school / by Shannon Berg
Description: Minneapolis, Minnesota : Abdo Publishing, 2021 | Series: Strong, healthy girls | Includes online resources and index.
Identifiers: ISBN 9781532192227 (lib. bdg.) | ISBN 9781098210120 (ebook)
Subjects: LCSH: Girls--Books and reading--Juvenile literature. | Girls--Life skills guides--Juvenile literature. | Bullying in schools--Juvenile literature. | High school student extra-curricular activities--Juvenile literature. | Interpersonal relations--Juvenile literature. | Social problems in education--Juvenile literature.
Classification: DDC 155.533--dc23

CONTENTS

DR. AMY

Dr. Amy Bellmore is fascinated by humans and inspired by teens. She works as a professor of human development in the Department of Educational Psychology at the University of Wisconsin–Madison, where she conducts research on the peer relationships of adolescents and teaches courses on adolescent development.

She earned a PhD in developmental psychology at the University of Connecticut. Though she did not declare a major in psychology until the middle of her sophomore year in college, she has evidence that she was destined to study teens from a work aptitude test she took her sophomore year in high school. Based on the results of the test about her interests and skills, she discovered that the best job for her was a research psychologist. Now that she has worked in that career for almost 20 years, she is happy to verify that the test was correct.

During her career, Dr. Amy has conducted numerous studies on the social experiences of teens, which are published in more than 60 articles and book chapters. Most of these studies take place through partnerships with public middle schools and high

CHAPTER ONE

THE GREAT BALANCING ACT

No doubt about it: if you ask any teenager what stresses her out about school, homework is likely to be somewhere near the top of the list. If you're among those who stress about homework, there may be different reasons for the stress. Sometimes you just have a lot to do. Other times, the assignment is really hard, and you don't understand it. Maybe the assignment came up suddenly and conflicts with something else in your schedule. Or worse yet, you totally forgot to do it, and now you're rushing to finish it. If you're a typical teen, you've probably been in most of these situations. Hopefully not all at the same time, but it can happen.

Handling your homework successfully is a balancing act. It takes effort to keep track of everything you have going on.

You can use tools such as a planner or an app on your phone to remind you when you have assignments due, but you're the one who has to make the time to do the work. That can be hard when you just want to relax with your friends or put it off one more day. Unfortunately, once you get behind, you may find it hard to catch up.

> More often than not, things work out better with a little planning.

Many people justify procrastination by saying that they work better under pressure or that they have something more important they have to do first. But then they find themselves cramming at the last minute. More often than not, things work out better with a little planning—as Emma found out the hard way.

EMMA'S STORY

Chester's Coffee Shop was busy on Wednesday afternoon when Emma and Sophia walked in to order their usual.

"I haven't started this week's English packet," Emma admitted as they sat down with their drinks. She pulled her homework from her backpack.

"Oh, I've only done the first page," Sophia said. "Do you want to work on it together?"

"Yeah. I can't be late again. I have to get it in on Friday this time."

The girls diligently talked about the first question in their packet for a few minutes. But then they spent more time swapping videos on their phones and taking selfies with their drinks than they did on homework. Before Emma knew it, her phone said it was ten to five.

"I gotta go," she said, throwing her stuff into her backpack. "I have to get to swim practice early tonight."

"Ugh," groaned Sophia. "Again?"

"I have a meet this weekend. Coach might let me swim the 200-meter butterfly if I can get my time down."

"Nice! I'll walk with you," Sophia said and followed Emma out the door.

**

After a long swimming practice, Emma slumped at the table as she ate a late dinner.

"You look tired," her dad commented. Emma just nodded.

"Do you have any homework to finish?" her mom asked.

"I worked on it with Sophia," Emma said, which was true. "But it's not due until Friday." Also true.

"You only have two days, then," her dad pointed out.

"I'll work on it in class. I'm almost done." Not as true.

Getting ready for bed, Emma looked at the barely started packet with "60 POINTS" printed in bold along the top. She had only received half the points on the last couple of packets, and they were dragging her grade down. She thought about trying to answer a few more questions, but she was so tired. She returned the packet to her backpack and went to bed.

**

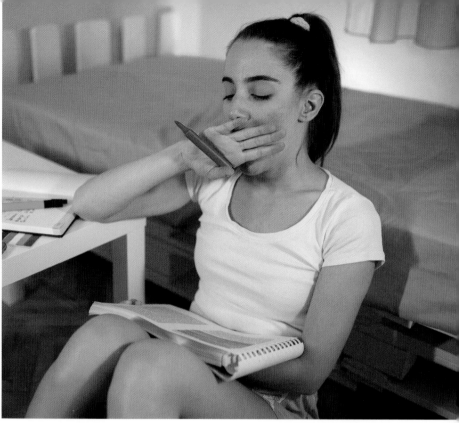

The next day, Emma didn't have any time in English class to work on her packet. Now she only had one day left to finish it. On the way home from school, Sophia asked whether she wanted to go to Chester's again, but Emma suggested they do their homework at her house instead.

"I still have a lot to do on the English packet before swim practice."

"OK. I finished mine last night, so I can help you."

"Thanks," Emma said.

TALK ABOUT IT

≡ **Are you a planner or a procrastinator?**

≡ **Have you ever put off doing something you knew you should do? What were the consequences?**

13

At home, they grabbed the cookie jar and sat down at the table. Sophia pulled out her algebra book. Emma had forgotten that she also had algebra homework that night.

They worked for the next hour, and Emma was nearly halfway through the packet. Even though Sophia helped her with the vocabulary words, Sophia kept stopping to check her phone or show Emma somebody's dumb picture. Emma just wanted to get

the packet done. *Maybe I can finish the rest after swimming*, she thought, just as her mom arrived home.

"What are you girls working on?" she asked as she put away a bag of groceries.

"I'm finishing my English packet," Emma answered.

"I hope so. I saw your grade on the last couple." Her mom peeked over at the table, then came in for a closer look.

"I'm almost done!" Emma tried to pull it away, but her mom just held out her hand.

"Let me see it, Emma." Her tone was no longer cheerful. Emma's cheeks went hot as she handed her mom the half-finished packet.

Emma's cheeks went hot as she handed her mom the half-finished packet.

"This is not almost done," she said, flipping through the pages. "You can't get this done before swimming."

"I can finish after," Emma argued.

"Sorry, but no. This thing is worth 60 points, and it's the third packet in a row you haven't finished. You have to stay home to finish this. No swimming tonight."

"Mom!" Emma blurted out. "If I'm not at practice, Coach Morris won't let me swim the butterfly!"

"That's tough. School comes first. Text your coach to let him know you can't make it tonight."

Emma's frustration was building to tears, and Sophia mouthed "sorry" across the table. Emma dropped her head on her arm so nobody would see her cry.

Later that night, Emma had finally finished her English packet and her algebra when she got a text from Coach Morris. "Too bad. We'll skip the butterfly this week." Her heart sank, but at least he was still letting her compete at the meet. And now she had a little more time to work on her butterfly stroke. She would make sure she competed in the butterfly at the next meet. Next time, she wouldn't let her homework hold her back.

TALK ABOUT IT

≡ Have you ever had two obligations at the same time? How did you handle it?

≡ What could Emma have done differently?

≡ What helps you balance your homework load? Do you use any tools to help you keep track of it?

ASK THE

EXPERT

Homework is one of your first encounters with work-life balance. Having a healthy work-life balance is a skill that can be a struggle even for adults. If you feel stressed out every time you think about your homework, that may be a sign you're becoming overwhelmed. Talk to your teachers, parents, or school counselor about ways to balance your work. Stress can actually make it harder for your brain to begin a project.

Many schools have resources for students who need help. Unexpected challenges such as family or health problems, homelessness, or food insecurity can make it hard to concentrate on school. Students facing these issues should talk to a school counselor right away. The school may be able to help. Many schools also have places for students to go after school for homework help. Even if you don't need help, you may find it useful to have the time set aside in a quiet place.

When possible, try to work ahead on your homework. You may have occasions when something out of your control comes up and you just can't fit in your homework. If you've already worked ahead, you'll be better able to handle those surprises. Avoid the temptation to wait until the last minute. You may underestimate the time you have to finish a task, which will only add to your stress level. Having high stress levels day after day will start to affect your health and only make it harder to do your work.

GET **HEALTHY**

- Make a plan for your homework. When can you set aside time? What do you need to prioritize?

- Find a tool to help you track your homework. You could use a journal, daily checklist, or even an app on your phone.

- Set your own homework routine. Create a study space. Give yourself a little incentive. Figure out what works for you.

- If you're struggling, ask for help. Don't wait until it's too late.

- Take care of yourself. Get enough sleep and eat regular meals. If you find yourself staying up late to get homework done, find a different time to do your work.

THE LAST WORD FROM **SHANNON**

Do you feel ready to take on your homework? Finding that perfect balance isn't easy, and you'll have times when you don't get it quite right. Everyone struggles with this sometimes. I know I sure did. I balanced school, band, and a part-time job. I definitely made mistakes, but I figured it out in the end. This is all part of the learning process. The important thing is to learn from your mistakes so that you have better results next time.

You'll rely on your ability to manage your time throughout your life. Whether in school, at home, or in a job, you'll need to find your balance. If you truly are one of the rare people who thrive under pressure, you may find yourself working in a high-stakes job, like an emergency room doctor or a firefighter. In the meantime, though, you still have to get your homework done.

"I don't think this is working," she finally admitted. "I just can't remember this stuff. I should probably just go home and reread the chapters," Liv said. "But thanks for reviewing with me."

"You know, I sit right next to you. If you were to glance over and see my paper, I wouldn't tell anyone," Jayden said.

"That's sweet, but if we get caught cheating, you'll get in trouble too."

"OK. Just sayin'."

***

Liv had a hard time sleeping that night. She had stayed up trying to read until her mother came in at midnight and confiscated her history book, demanding she go to bed. Liv forced herself to lie in bed, trying to calm her anxiety about the test. Why hadn't she paid more attention in class? Why hadn't she taken better notes?

TALK ABOUT IT

- What is your favorite method of studying and why?
- Do you ever study with friends, or do you prefer to do it on your own?
- How would you react if someone offered to help you cheat?

> Liv forced herself to lie in bed, trying to calm her anxiety about the test.

***

The test was as hard as Liv feared, and she caught herself looking over at Jayden. He didn't look at her, but he kept his paper out in the open. She would just need to glance down. But she

TALK ABOUT IT

= Do you get nervous before tests? If so, how do you relax?

= Why do you think Liv's mom forced Liv to quit studying and go to bed? Do you agree with her mom's decision?

didn't want to take the chance of getting Jayden in trouble. She focused on her own paper. She struggled, but she found she knew more answers than she expected.

That night, she and Jayden decided to go out for pizza to celebrate being done with the test. Just as she took her first bite, her phone dinged, and then Jayden's did as well.

"Grades," they both said and grabbed their phones.

"How did you do?" Jayden asked.

"I got a B-plus!" Liv cheered. Jayden high-fived her. She would have to wait to see whether it was enough to get her a C in the class, but it still felt good.

ASK THE

EXPERT

There are ways to deal with anxiety around tests and failing grades that can help you get through it all. Of course, starting with good study habits from the beginning of the class will help you avoid feeling the pinch later. Study basics include active listening, active reading, and reviewing your work. Active learners ask questions, take notes, and organize the information so they can use it later. Review helps you reaffirm what you know and fills in any gaps you find. When studying for tests, the key is to find what works for you.

As for the test itself, try to relax. Briefly look over the entire test before you start, and answer the easiest questions first. Fill in all multiple-choice questions. A guess is better than a blank space. Review your answers. As long as you do your best, you have something to be proud of.

Liv was certainly anxious about her test, but that anxiety didn't quite rise to the level of test anxiety. Test anxiety is a condition that can cause physical symptoms. A moderate amount of stress makes us more alert and helps us do our best. But, as in the case of test anxiety, too much stress has a negative effect on our bodies and minds. This stress level can make it harder to learn and perform well.

Cheating may seem like a quick fix, but it can have long-term consequences. Even if you don't get caught, you put yourself even farther behind your classmates and cheat yourself out of an education. Not to mention how unfair it is to your classmates who earned their grades honestly.

GET HEALTHY

- Don't cram for a test. People learn best from repeated exposure to the same ideas.

- Gather all your information in one place to make sure you don't miss anything important. Actively review your information.

- Take breaks as you study, and get plenty of sleep.

- If your grade is in trouble, talk to your teacher.

- If you have serious anxiety that results in physical symptoms, talk to your doctor about treatment.

THE LAST WORD FROM SHANNON

In high school, I was a pretty good student. But algebra was just not my subject, and I struggled all year. I knew I had to get an A on the final exam or risk not passing the class. I made the extra effort and studied harder than I ever had—and I managed to pull it off. I was prouder of my C in algebra than many of the As I received in other classes.

If you have several low grades and cannot seem to catch up, you probably need some outside help. Don't be afraid to ask your teacher, look for a tutor, or find resources to help you get organized. Sometimes you just need to put in the extra time. Your education is worth the extra effort.

CHAPTER THREE

LEARNING FROM LEARNING DISABILITIES

Some students may struggle in school in ways that go beyond failing a test here or there. These students may have one or more learning disabilities. Chances are good that you or someone you know has some type of learning disability. The term *learning disability* describes a condition in which a person has trouble with a certain type of learning or neurological processing. Some doctors refer to learning disabilities as learning differences. Many types of learning differences have nothing to do with how smart someone is. In fact, to be diagnosed with a learning disability, a person must have average intelligence or higher.

Dyslexia is one of the most common learning disabilities and may be found in as many as one in five kids. Dyslexia describes a difficulty with the brain's ability to recognize letters

If you have
a learning
disability,
make sure
you recognize
your strengths
and find
the support
you need.

or numbers or both, which can lead to problems with reading and math.

Kids with attention deficit hyperactivity disorder (ADHD) face unique challenges. Their brains fail to filter information coming in or going out, which makes it difficult to focus on a single thing. Some also have a hard time sitting still because their bodies have too much energy. As many as 8 percent of kids have ADHD, and many kids have both ADHD and dyslexia.

If you have a learning disability, make sure you recognize your strengths and find the support you need. If you don't have a learning disability, there are ways you can support those who do. Be there for them, and don't assume you know what they are capable of based on their disability. Maddie's classmates think they know what kind of student she is, but she surprises them.

MADDIE'S STORY

Maddie searched the room. Everyone was huddling in groups, and no one looked at her. Even her friends left her standing alone. Mrs. Greenwald leaned over Maddie's shoulder.

"It looks like Max and Claire's group still needs one more person. Why don't you join them?" she said. Maddie nodded and headed into Max's group. Normally she would be really excited to do a project on ancient Egyptian history. She had always loved everything about ancient Egypt. But group projects were the worst.

Claire rolled her eyes as Maddie walked up. Maddie tried to ignore her. "Mrs. Greenwald said I should join you guys."

"Yeah, OK," Max said without enthusiasm.

"Fine, but we have to have this done by Monday," Claire said.

"I know," Maddie said. She didn't blame Claire, exactly. Maddie had trouble getting assignments turned in on time, and her classmates had noticed. Her ADHD made it hard for her to finish homework. Her 504 plan at school gave her extra time to do work, but she didn't want to tell Claire and Max about it. She just wanted to be treated like one of the group for once.

"Now remember, you need to come up with a display for the topic on your card by Monday. Be as creative as you want," Mrs. Greenwald said.

> Maddie had trouble getting assignments turned in on time. . . . Her ADHD made it hard for her to finish homework.

Max unfolded the paper listing their assignment. "Mummification," he read.

Maddie couldn't help smiling. "I love mummies," she said.

"Well, I have a trifold at home we can use for the display," Claire said. She and Max talked about what notes to include in the display. Claire offered to print the notes, and Max said he would get her the research. Any time Maddie tried to add something to the conversation, they talked over her.

Class was almost over when Maddie finally asked, "What do you want me to do?"

Max shrugged. "You could do some artwork to make it look nice, I guess."

"Yeah, just print out some pictures or something," Claire added.

***

On Sunday afternoon, Maddie looked at the pile of paper and string on the dining room table. She had made a pretty big mess, but she still felt satisfied with the result. She had been working on her display almost nonstop for two days.

Her dad walked in and laughed. "Is this your mummy project?" he asked.

"Yep. Think you can give me a ride to school tomorrow?"

"I don't know how else you'll get that there. Now clear the table for dinner."

Maddie dragged her display to the front door, leaving a trail of crepe paper in her wake. Claire texted her, "Is your art ready for the display?"

"Yes."

"I left a spot on the board for it."

"It won't fit on the board. I've got it."

"If you say so."

Maddie could tell Claire didn't believe she had her part of the project ready. She couldn't stop herself from texting, "Did you and Max get the notes done?"

Claire didn't respond.

***

On Monday morning, Maddie brought her art project into class. Mrs. Greenwald gave her a smile. Everyone stared, including Max and Claire, but Maddie just set her project next to her desk until her group was called to present. Claire unfolded her board with notes

TALK ABOUT IT

= **Do you think Claire and Max treated Maddie fairly? Why do you think that?**

= **How might having a learning disability make group projects difficult?**

printed in fancy fonts pasted onto colorful paper. She and Max took turns reading the notes, then looked at Mrs. Greenwald.

"I would like to hear from Maddie about her creation," she said.

Maddie had laid her life-size, bisected mummy on the table. From head to toe, she had packed her crepe paper creation with different colors. She explained to the class where the Egyptians would remove certain organs, what they would replace them with, and how each body part was wrapped.

Kids started raising their hands to ask her questions. Then one student asked whether he could come up to look

at it. Before she knew it, the table was surrounded with people checking out her mummy's innards.

"Did you make this by yourself?" Mrs. Greenwald asked. Max and Claire stood behind their board, watching her.

"Well," she said. "It was a group project."

Afterward, Max shuffled up to Maddie. "You did a really great job," he said, looking at the mummy. "This is really cool."

"Thanks," Maddie replied.

"I'm sorry we didn't, you know, help with it."

"You did your part."

"Yeah, but we should've been working together," Max admitted.

Maddie nodded. "That would have been nice."

TALK ABOUT IT

≡ **Have you ever worked really hard on a project you were passionate about? How did it feel?**

≡ **Why do you think Maddie gave Max and Claire credit for helping? Would you have done that?**

≡ **What could Max and Claire have done differently?**

ASK THE

EXPERT

Students with ADHD, such as Maddie, may have a hard time focusing, but their lack of filter can allow them to come up with incredibly creative ideas. Those with ADHD also have a flip side to the lack of focus, called hyperfocus. With hyperfocus, they zero in on a subject in which they have a lot of interest. Maddie had an interest in mummies and was able to focus her attention on a very creative visual display for the project.

The typical classroom was created for typical kids, and this can make it difficult for students with learning differences. Whether you have a learning disability or not, remember to celebrate your strengths.

Researchers predict that the portion of students with learning disabilities who are also gifted with talent, creativity, or high intelligence is actually much higher than previously thought. So as someone with a learning disability, even if you feel frustrated, behind, or confused during class, remember that you're just as smart as other students. And although you've struggled with certain aspects of learning, you've excelled in others.

If you don't have a learning disability but have classmates who do, keep in mind that they have gifts to offer. Remember that they often have to work much harder to get the same result as you and may need extra time. But that doesn't mean that they don't have a lot to contribute. If you turn your back on them, you could miss out on a unique perspective you won't find anywhere else.

GET HEALTHY

- Find the academic support you need. You may need classroom accommodations or special instruction.

- Be your own advocate. Explain what you need.

- Learn more about what makes your brain different. You'll find coping strategies and ways to focus on your positive traits.

- Be supportive and inclusive of those who have learning differences.

THE LAST WORD FROM SHANNON

As a parent of two teenagers with learning disabilities, I understand the struggles that kids go through in school socially, emotionally, and academically. Being excluded from group projects is just one example of their experiences. They have also had to learn to advocate for themselves with teachers who didn't follow their 504 plan or when they simply needed extra help. They have struggled with finding the right balance of therapies and medications. In the end, though, they are bright and talented, and I know they can accomplish anything they decide to do.

Every student is unique, whether you have a learning disability or not. Your superpower is whatever makes you unique. It gives you strength and allows you to see the world in your own way. Take pride in the things that make you who you are. Just like you, they are a gift.

CHAPTER FOUR

BENCHED

After-school activities can make school a better experience for many kids. After all, you get to choose what you're doing, and it can be a lot more fun than most of your classes. One of the joys of getting older is trying new things and meeting new people. For some people, though, building up the courage to try something new is a real challenge.

If that is you, I encourage you to take that challenge. You have little to lose and so much to gain. Whether your interest lies in sports, music, drama, or chess club, you can gain a sense of community, make new friends, and learn valuable skills such as teamwork, integrity, and perseverance.

Perhaps you fear you won't be good enough. Maybe you're afraid you won't make the team or get the role you wanted in the school play. Remember that everyone starts at the beginning. Even if it doesn't turn out to be the experience you were expecting, you can learn a lot from that too.

RUBY'S STORY

Shae stood on her tiptoes and shot the basketball at the hoop in Ruby's driveway. It teetered on the rim but dropped off the side.

"Dang it." Shae sighed. "I'm never going to make the team."

"Don't be silly," Ruby replied, dribbling the ball. "You're great. You just made that shot from the street a few minutes ago. I wonder if we'll make the varsity team."

"I'll just be happy to make any team."

Ruby turned and shot. The ball fell through the net. She did a small victory hop before tossing the ball back to Shae. "We'll be great," Ruby assured her friend.

* * *

"Whoa," Ruby and Shae said in unison when they walked into the gym. Dozens of girls were dribbling basketballs, passing to each other, blocking, and taking shots. They knew a few girls from their middle school team, but most of them were strangers. Tall strangers.

TALK ABOUT IT

= **Why do you think Shae is nervous?**

= **Have you ever been nervous to try out for something?**

= **How would you prepare to try out for a team or audition for a part?**

> She did a small victory hop before tossing the ball back to Shae. "We'll be great," Ruby assured her friend.

47

"There are so many of them," Shae said, stating the obvious.

"We're just as good as they are," Ruby told Shae, but she wasn't sure she believed it herself. These girls were good. "Let's warm up," Ruby suggested.

The tryouts were long and hard. They ran, played one-on-one, and threw free throws. It seemed to go on forever. By the end, Ruby was exhausted.

"That was harder than our hardest game in middle school," Shae said as they left. Ruby could only nod.

* * *

TALK ABOUT IT

= **Have you ever been one of the younger people in a group? What was it like?**

= **Why do you think the tryouts were harder than Ruby was expecting?**

= **Do you think Ruby left the tryouts as confident as she went in?**

The team lists were posted online the next morning. Ruby scanned the varsity list but didn't find her name. She had to scan all the way down the junior varsity team list, but there she was. At least she had made the team, and so had Shae.

Their first practice was the next day after school. Ruby tried to shake off the tough tryouts, but she was still a little sore. There was more running, blocking, passing, and free throw drills. For two weeks, each practice was the same—a lot of work. As the first game grew closer, their coach started splitting them into two sides to play against

each other. Ruby wasn't rotated in as often as some of the other girls, including Shae. She tried not to let it get to her. She also tried not to dwell on the fact that she had a few inches on Shae and some of the other girls, so she thought she would make a better forward.

She tried not to let it get to her.

* * *

On the day of the first game, Ruby felt like the coach wasn't giving her a fair shot. She was discouraged, but she also didn't want that to ruin her first high school game. She decided she could still make the game fun, even if she didn't get to play as much as she wanted. And she really liked her teammates.

The team members boarded the bus to drive across the city to the school they were playing. Ruby shared the cookies her mom had made and even started everyone singing the school song. Shae was used to Ruby's extra energy, so she just laughed.

"What?" Ruby asked her afterward.

"Nothing," Shae said. "Just save some of that energy for the game."

"We have to get pumped up," Ruby protested. "Girls JV doesn't have cheerleaders, so

> She was discouraged, but she also didn't want to ruin her first high school game.

TALK ABOUT IT

= **Have you ever been disappointed with how your role on a team or in a group turned out? Did you stick with it or drop out?**

= **What do you think changed Ruby's attitude about her role on the team?**

= **Have you ever watched a friend do better than you? How did you feel?**

I guess we have to cheer ourselves on. Besides, I probably won't play much."

Ruby did spend a lot of time on the sidelines during the game, but she didn't let that stop her from cheering everyone else on. By the last ten minutes, she had only rotated in for a few plays. When Shae made a three-point shot, Ruby leaped up and down, yelling. They were up by eight points.

"OK, Ruby, go finish out the game," the coach said with a smile.

"Really?" Ruby asked.

"Hustle!" the coach yelled, so Ruby rushed to replace Shae. As they passed each other, Ruby high-fived Shae. "Way to shoot it from the street," she told her friend.

EXPERT

Participating in activities outside of school can help you express yourself, relieve stress, and even help you strengthen your mind. A strong interest in something can help you build your self-confidence. But putting yourself out there can feel risky because you don't want to fail. You might be worried that you'll find yourself at the bottom of the pack. Just remember that most people are not great at something the first time they try it. The only way to get better at something is to get out there and do it.

Even if you've done something before, you can always reach a new level. Ruby had been on her middle school's basketball team, but even the JV high school team was a huge new challenge. On the new team, Ruby had great players surrounding her who would help her improve. She was also learning a new level of hard work.

Look for activities that give you a spark of joy just for participating in them. As long as you're having fun, you shouldn't be too worried about whether you're in a supporting role or the starring role. A positive attitude will make a good impression on those in charge too. Next time, they may give you more responsibility and a little more recognition.

GET **HEALTHY**

- When things don't go the way you want them to, look at it as an opportunity to grow. Watch the people who did get that part you wanted. What can you learn from them to help you next time around?

- Persistence pays off. Keep practicing and working for what you want, and you'll see improvement.

- Enjoy the ride. You don't have to be the best at something to find the joy in it.

- Be a gracious winner. When you get your chance to be the star, remember how it felt to be on the other side, and be kind to those who are facing disappointment. You may be their role model now.

THE LAST WORD FROM **SHANNON**

After-school activities are a great way to do something fun with your friends. You may even discover your passion. And if an activity is a really bad fit, then at least you discovered something you can cross off your list. You can say that you tried it and that it wasn't for you.

We tend to enjoy things more the better we are at them. Just don't give up too soon. Remember that improvement takes time and effort. Even if you're not the star player, you still have the benefit of meeting new people, learning new skills, and expanding your mind. So give it a little time before moving on to the next activity. In the end, find an activity that you want to do because it makes you happy, no matter how many lines you have or how much time you get on the court.

CHAPTER FIVE

PAVE YOUR OWN PATH

"What kind of career do you want?" "What are your plans after high school?" You probably hear things like these all the time—especially at school. Today's teenagers are pressured to think about their careers at a younger age than previous generations. How in the world are you supposed to know what you want to do with your entire life at this age?

I'm going to let you in on a secret. You don't have to. You may be surprised to read that. Don't get me wrong. Goals and life plans are important. But there are many kinds of goals, and you don't need to map out your entire life right now.

As a teen, you're developing your identity. Your life is all about opening doors, not closing them. Explore your options and never assume that a certain path isn't possible for you. Keeping doors open means always doing your best in school and activities so you can take them wherever you decide to go, whether that means college, a vocational school, or starting on a career path.

> *When people push you toward a path that isn't right for you, remember that they probably have the best intentions at heart.*

You may change your mind several times in the next few years, and that's OK. As long as you keep those doors open, you'll be ready for anything.

When people push you toward a path that isn't right for you, remember that they probably have the best intentions at heart but that you need to forge your own way. Maria discovered that this takes courage.

MARIA'S STORY

Maria and her parents sat down with Maria's counselor, Ms. Ellison, in her tiny office.

"Thank you for meeting with us," her mother said. "We are very concerned about the classes Maria will take next year."

"Tell me what concerns you," Ms. Ellison said.

"Well, next year is her junior year, and then she applies for college. We want her to take the right classes," Maria's dad explained.

"Maria's grades are excellent, and she has great extracurriculars," Ms. Ellison told him. She then turned to Maria.

"I know your robotics team did really well at regionals this year, and a lot of people think that was because of you."

Maria smiled at the memory. She loved making the machine do what it was supposed to do and figuring out the problems when something went wrong.

"You know, you'll have more room for electives next year," Ms. Ellison added. "Were you thinking of taking the advanced robotics class?"

TALK ABOUT IT

- **If you could take any class, what would it be? Why?**
- **What is your favorite activity? Can you picture doing it as a job?**
- **Why do you think Maria's parents want her to become a doctor?**

Maria started to answer, but her mom jumped in. "She needs to take Latin."

"It will be a big help when she gets to medical school," her dad added. Why her parents thought she should go to medical school was a total mystery to Maria. Just because she got good grades in science didn't mean she wanted to be a doctor. Her excitement about junior year fell.

"You can already include robotics on your college applications. You don't need the advanced robotics class," her father told her.

***

Just because she got good grades in science didn't mean she wanted to be a doctor.

By the next Monday, Maria still hadn't figured out what to do about her classes. She stopped back at Ms. Ellison's office, hoping she could help. The meeting started out easily enough as they looked over Maria's grades.

"Well, you should definitely think about AP classes for

next year," Ms. Ellison said. Maria nodded along. She already figured that much. "And you qualify for precalculus. That still leaves you an elective. Have you given it more thought?"

"Yeah, but my parents still want me to take Latin," Maria mumbled, fiddling with her backpack zipper.

TALK ABOUT IT

▪ Many children talk about what they want to be when they grow up. Which careers can you remember wanting to do when you were younger? Have they changed?

▪ Do you feel pressured to make decisions now about your life after high school? If so, how does it make you feel?

"Is medical school something you want to do?"

Maria shrugged. "I don't know. I mean, I know being a doctor is a good job, and they want me to have a good job."

"Being a doctor is a great job, and I'm sure your parents want you to have a good job, but that doesn't answer my question."

"I don't know if I want to be a doctor," Maria admitted.

"What class would you take if you could take any of them?" Ms. Ellison asked.

"Robotics," Maria said without hesitating. Ms. Ellison smiled.

"I think it's great you're thinking about college. But medical school would be a long way off. You have plenty of time to decide. And most people don't take Latin until college, if they take it at all," Ms. Ellison said.

"What do you think I should do?" Maria asked.

"As long as you keep studying hard and getting good grades, you'll be ready

> "What class would you take if you could take any of them?"

TALK ABOUT IT

- Has anyone ever inspired you to follow a dream? Who was it? What was the dream?

- Do you think Maria's parents will agree to her staying in robotics? Why or why not?

- What is something you can do to keep your options open after high school?

for college. You should also do things that interest you, though. You never know where that could take you."

"What about my parents?" Maria asked. "They don't even want me to be on the robotics team next year."

"Remind your parents that the robotics program is an excellent source of college scholarships," Ms. Ellison said with a wink. Maria smiled for the first time all day.

ASK THE

EXPERT

There's a reason schools encourage kids to plan for their futures. In the past, many young people graduating from high school simply lacked the basic skills to decide what they wanted to do for a living. Others arrived at college unprepared for college life and college academics. With the price of college tuition, that can be a costly mistake. Schools felt the need to better prepare graduating students for their next steps. So they put more of an emphasis on preparing for college and future careers.

Unfortunately, some kids end up feeling pushed in one direction without really understanding their options. Don't be afraid to explore beyond what you know to discover your own path. Rather than focusing on what you want to do when you grow up, focus on setting goals that feel meaningful and rewarding along the way.

So how do you create your path? At this stage of your life, the important skills for you to learn are how to set a goal, plan the necessary steps to achieve that goal, and follow through. You can have short- and long-term goals. Start with smaller steps you can achieve in the near future. Think about why you want to reach this goal and what it will do for you—not your parents, your teachers, or anyone else. How will achieving this goal help *you*?

GET HEALTHY

- Stay involved in extracurricular activities. Even if those activities don't ultimately lead to a career, you may gain a lifelong hobby that makes you happy.

- Find your passion. Talk to teachers and school counselors about your ideas. You can explore different career paths by shadowing someone in a profession you're interested in.

- Celebrate your successes—no matter how small the victory. And don't forget to thank the mentor who helped you get there.

- Celebrate your failures. Every failure helps you grow. Learn from your mistakes and create new goals and new paths.

THE LAST WORD FROM SHANNON

Planning your future is a daunting task. When I was in school, I worried about having a stable job, so I planned on becoming a lawyer. I just assumed my passion for writing couldn't pay the bills and never explored jobs for writers. I closed that door, and it took me years to realize that there are many careers for writers. Closing that door was a mistake.

Remember that you're in charge of your future. Explore your options and don't assume anything is off-limits to you. Just because nobody in your family or neighborhood has ever done something doesn't mean that you can't be the first. Your family wants what is best for you, but once you're an adult, you'll be the one who decides just what that is.

CHAPTER SIX

MAKING AN IMPRESSION

Making a good first impression can go a long way with your teachers, but what can you do if you make a bad first impression or you just don't get along? With all the teachers you'll have in your life, you're bound to have one or two whom you just don't get along with. This will be true throughout your life. Sometimes you have to learn to work with people you don't like.

Don't give up, though. There is a good chance you can improve your relationship with your teacher. Don't start an argument, but be honest in a polite way. If you think you might have done something wrong, be the first to apologize. You can also tell the teacher how you feel. Sometimes honesty is the best way to make a connection with your teacher and advocate for yourself. Lily learned that a teacher's first impression doesn't have to be the only impression.

LILY'S STORY

Lily ran down the hallway and pushed her way through door 201.
Everyone else was already sitting down, watching the teacher.

"Sorry," Lily said before grabbing an open seat in the back.
From a few rows over, her friend Zoey raised her eyebrows. Lily
shrugged. She had gotten her schedule mixed up and went to the
wrong room first before she realized she was supposed to be in
biology class.

"OK," her teacher said. "I think you're doing pretty well."

"You do?"

"Sure. You did well on the quiz. Are you having a problem?"

Mrs. Idleman looked confused.

"Actually, I was wondering if, well, maybe you don't like me?" Lily managed to squeak out.

Mrs. Idleman frowned. "Why would you think that?"

"Well, I was late to class the first day, and I know you don't like my brother, and you didn't write 'good job' on my paper the way you did for Sam's, and you never call on me, but that's

not really fair because I'm not my brother." Lily felt a little out of breath.

"Wow," said Mrs. Idleman. "I guess I didn't realize all of that. I mean, your brother isn't one of my fonder memories, I will admit. But I didn't mean to give you the impression that I don't like you."

Lily wasn't sure what else to say except, "OK."

"Thank you for letting me know," Mrs. Idleman said. "What do you say we start over?"

Lily smiled. "Sure. Do I still get to keep the A on my quiz?"

Mrs. Idleman smiled back. "I think that would be fair."

ASK THE

EXPERT

How can you reset the impression a teacher has of you? First of all, don't give up and assume you can never get along. Let your teacher get to know you, and get to know your teacher. Teachers want to see you succeed. That is why they got into the profession in the first place. The more they get to know you and understand that you really are trying, the more likely they are to help you.

Remember that your teacher is a person too. He or she is far from perfect, just like everyone else. Teachers do make mistakes and have biases. It's OK to point out when they are wrong, but remember to do it respectfully. Learning to speak up and advocate for yourself with your teachers is a valuable skill. Together you can figure out a way to work together.

Ask your teacher if you can talk at a time when you won't be rushed. Don't try to have a conversation two minutes before the bell rings to start class. While talking, show your teacher you're taking the situation seriously. Make eye contact and actually listen.

If you still feel like you're not getting anywhere with your teacher, talk to your guidance counselor at school. Your counselor may have other tips for getting along with that particular teacher. Your teacher will appreciate you trying these steps on your own before going to your parents for help. Of course, if your teacher is doing something inappropriate such as discriminating against you, go straight to your counselor and parents to report it.

GET **HEALTHY**

- Show up to class. If you miss a day, it is your responsibility to find out what you missed and to make up the work.

- Show you care about the class. Use good manners, take notes, and ask questions.

- Put yourself in your teacher's shoes. How would you want students to act if you were teaching?

- Realize that every teacher does things differently. Learn what is important to each teacher.

- If your teacher does something that upsets you, think of reasons why your teacher may have acted that way.

THE LAST WORD FROM **SHANNON**

Will your teacher be your new best friend? Maybe not, but your teacher can help you in many ways that you may not have considered. Teachers can advise you on which course in that subject you should take next, recommend you for other educational opportunities, and write college recommendation letters. Don't underestimate the importance of your teachers!

You have every reason to try to improve your relationship with a difficult teacher, and you have very little to lose. Think of it as practice for adult life when you may have a boss you don't get along with. You'll always have to deal with people you find difficult. You might as well learn how to make it work now.

crush since seventh grade, much less tried to kiss him. "Why would Amelia say that?"

"Oh, so you're saying you didn't?"

"I'm saying I barely know Drew, and I have never even come close to trying to kiss him." Keesha tried to keep her voice from rising but was having

TALK ABOUT IT

= How have you handled a day you just didn't want to go to school and face everyone? What worked for you? Why do you think it helped?

= Have any of your friends ever had a fight that forced you to choose sides? How did you decide?

= Why do you think Amelia lied about Keesha? Has a friend ever lied about you?

a hard time. Why would Amelia lie about her? Was she trying to justify dumping her?

"Well, Amelia says you did," Lara said, but she didn't seem as convinced. She slipped past Keesha, out of the bathroom.

***

Keesha entered English lit class in a daze, still trying to figure out what was happening.

"Hey, Keesha," Abby said as she took her seat. She was kind of funny and always friendly. Now she was tilting her head at

Keesha with furrowed brows. "What's wrong?"

Keesha realized she was moping and tried to shake it off. She didn't really want to talk about it. "I'm fine."

Abby looked her over like she wasn't buying it, but she didn't call Keesha out. Instead, she went in a totally unexpected direction.

"You know, you were awesome reading the part of Juliet in class the other day."

Keesha smiled for the first time all day. "Really?"

"Really. Have you ever been in a play?" Abby asked. Keesha shook her head.

"You should totally try out for the fall play. Do you want to come with me after school?"

"I don't know," Keesha said. She wasn't feeling very sociable, but reading the part in class had been kind of fun.

TALK ABOUT IT

- How do you think Abby made Keesha feel by talking to her?

- Think of a time when a kind gesture from someone made all the difference when you were feeling bad. Does that person know what it meant to you? Did you ever thank him or her?

Keesha realized she was moping and tried to shake it off. She didn't really want to talk about it.

"Just come check it out. If you decide you don't want to audition, you can join the stage crew with me. That's what I do. You get to run around with a headset and tell people what to do," Abby said with a laugh.

Maybe having something to do after school would help get her mind off her problems. And Abby seemed cool. "I guess it couldn't hurt to check it out."

* * *

A few weeks later, Keesha was walking to her locker before heading off to help Abby paint set pieces. Amelia and Lara were straight ahead, and Keesha had no choice but to walk right past them. Lara gave her a small smile, but Amelia gave her no more than a glance. Keesha was surprised to find that it hurt less than she expected.

CHAPTER EIGHT

TOXIC HALLWAYS

School bullies have probably been around since, well, the beginning of school. That's no excuse for their behavior, though. And it's certainly no comfort if you become a victim.

In the past, bullying often consisted of physical harassment, name-calling, and vicious gossip. Those things still exist, of course, but today, bullies have an efficient new tool at their disposal: social media. When bullying happens online, it can happen all day, every day—never giving the victim any rest.

Be on the lookout for bullying. Bullying is different from teasing in a few ways. First, bullies usually have more power than the victim, either because they are bigger, stronger, or more popular. Bullies set out to purposefully hurt the victims, either physically, emotionally, or socially. They also repeat their behavior over time.

Bullies always seem to pick out people who appear different from everyone else, thinking they make easy targets. But you

don't have to be an easy target. There are ways to defend yourself against bullies. When Amira became the target of a bully, her friends helped her figure it out.

AMIRA'S STORY

Amira stayed behind when everyone else got up to leave. Fatima looked over her shoulder.

"Aren't you coming?" she asked Amira.

Amira looked down at her phone in her lap and bit her lip. She felt sick. Dylan had posted on her page again. She held up her phone for Fatima to read. "Go back where you came from," it read.

"I don't want to see him in the hall," Amira admitted. Dylan's locker was only three down from hers. He always stared at her when she walked by, and it made her uncomfortable.

"I'll come with you," Fatima said, finally convincing Amira to get up from her seat. Fatima straightened her headscarf and picked up her books.

"You know, you should show that to the principal," Fatima said as they left the classroom.

"I just want to delete it. I don't want anyone seeing that."

"Don't delete it. Then you can't show anyone. I learned that the hard way."

"I don't want to show anyone! I just want him to leave me alone," Amira said.

"What does that even mean, 'Go back where you came from'?" Fatima said, getting angrier. "Where does he think you're from? You were born right here. Just because you wear a headscarf doesn't mean

TALK ABOUT IT

- Have you ever been targeted like Amira was? If so, how did it make you feel?
- If you were Amira, what would you do about the posts Dylan made?

"I don't want to show anyone! I just want him to leave me alone."

95

you don't belong here. I swear, some people's stupidity." Fatima started texting furiously on her phone.

When they reached Amira's locker, sure enough, Dylan was just down the row. Amira tried to get her books without him seeing her but had no such luck.

"Hey, ISIS," he said while walking away.

Amira's lip trembled, but she didn't want to cry in the middle of the hallway. "I think I'm going to go to the counselor's office," she told Fatima.

"OK, I'll walk with you."

* * *

Fatima left Amira at the office. Amira told the counselor what Dylan had said and showed her the post. The counselor listened sympathetically but didn't promise that Dylan would be punished.

"Just try to ignore him," she told Amira. "Kids like that are looking for attention."

None of that made Amira feel any better. She didn't think this was how the counselor was supposed to respond. By the time she left the counselor's office, the last class was about to let out, and she had to get her stuff to go home. That meant a trip back to her locker again. Her stomach felt knotted and hot.

* * *

When she got to her row of lockers, Amira was surprised to see Fatima and five other friends waiting for her. She almost cried

TALK ABOUT IT

= Do you think the counselor's advice was helpful? What else could she have said?

= How do you think Amira feels right now?

= Have you ever had to face a bully? If so, how did you handle it?

= What would you do if you saw someone being bullied? What rules does your school have about bullying? Whom should you report it to?

again, but this time because she was so grateful. She didn't have to face Dylan alone.

"We're going to be your entourage until Dylan stops being a jerk," Fatima said.

"That could mean forever," added Sam, and Amira laughed.

"Thanks, you guys," Amira said.

Amira opened her locker when Dylan's voice made her cringe.

"Hey, why do you wear that thing, anyway?" Dylan asked, pointing to Amira's headscarf. "You hiding a bomb under there?" He reached over to grab the headscarf. Even though Amira stepped back, Dylan almost managed to get his hand on it. Sam stepped between them just in time.

"I don't think so," said Sam.

"Is there a problem here?" Principal Nelson was standing behind the group.

"Yeah," said Fatima. "Dylan tried to pull Amira's headscarf off her and asked if she had a bomb under it."

"Is this true?" Mr. Nelson looked at Dylan, but Fatima answered.

"You want to see it recorded on my phone?" she asked.

"I definitely think I should look at that, but first I need to have a talk with Dylan." Mr. Nelson led Dylan off toward the office.

"I don't know what I would do without you guys," Amira said. "Thanks."

Fatima gave her shoulder a squeeze. "You would do the same for us."

ASK THE

EXPERT

School should be a safe space. Anytime you're singled out and harassed for your race, nationality, religion, gender, or disability, that is discrimination. Discrimination is illegal and should never be tolerated, especially at school. Schools are required to protect students from bullying and harassment based on discrimination. Unfortunately, some schools still struggle to find the best ways to do this and don't always react the way you wish they would.

Tell a parent or adult family member what is happening. You should also report all bullying to a teacher, counselor, or school administrator. Schools certainly can't do anything about a problem they are not aware of. However, school intervention can only do so much. Teenagers care more about social acceptance. That means social pressure is much more likely to effectively stop a bully than punishment from a school administrator.

Bullying prevention experts say that the best way to stop a bully is for kids to stick up for each other. This isn't always easy. Often, kids are worried about being the bully's next target, so they're tempted to say nothing or even join in with the bully. Speaking up takes courage. You risk becoming a target. When you think about what it feels like to be bullied, however, you know you don't want others to feel that way. That makes it a risk worth taking.

100

GET **HEALTHY**

- Do your best to ignore bullies. They are looking for a specific type of response, and if you don't give it to them, they will try elsewhere. This is especially important for cyberbullying.

- If you're being cyberbullied, don't delete posts before showing an adult. You may need them as evidence later.

- Make a pact with your friends. Agree to defend each other. The more friends you have sticking up for you, the better.

- React with positive social pressure. Speaking up is good, but starting an insult war will only make things worse.

- Practice with a friend or adult what to say when a bully attacks.

THE LAST WORD FROM **SHANNON**

Nobody deserves to be bullied at school. If you're being bullied, remember that it isn't about you or anything you did. Bullies are often kids who are having problems, either at home, in school, or in their personal lives. That doesn't excuse their behavior, but it may help you not take it quite as personally.

Standing up to a bully can be scary and difficult, especially if that bully is one of your friends. But staying quiet only gives that person your unspoken approval to keep behaving in an abusive way. The good news is that you don't have to stand up to these people alone. Surrounding yourself with positive people who will stand up for each other can lower your chances of being a victim, and you might end up preventing a bully from targeting someone else.

A SECOND
LOOK

Your high school years are a time of constant change and growth. You'll have good times and hard times along the way. Some classes may cause you nothing but stress, while others will inspire you. Whether you struggle to finish homework or want to try out for the school play, school always holds new challenges for you.

You may feel like you're the only person in the world going through whatever you're facing, but remember that you're not alone. Even if your friends aren't going through the same struggles as you, many other girls somewhere out there definitely are. This book has only touched on some of the most common issues keeping girls from success in school—things that happen to many girls every day.

Don't forget that school is also a place for fun. You'll meet new people and try new things. You'll explore new possibilities and make new friends. Even when you're stressed about a test or about whether you'll get that solo in choir, don't forget to enjoy the good things along the way.

If you ask for it, you'll find help either at home, from friends, or within your school. Part of growing into an adult is learning to stand up for yourself, to ask for what you need, and to take responsibility for yourself and your future. If you can manage to do those things, you'll crack the code to success in school.

XOXO,
SHANNON

PAY IT

FORWARD

Surviving and thriving at school is all about growth. Discovering what makes you feel your best is a journey that changes throughout your life. Now that you know what to focus on, you can pay it forward to a friend too. Remember the Get Healthy tips throughout this book, and then take these steps to get healthy and get going.

1. Homework doesn't have to be the bane of your existence. Track your homework in a way that works for you. There are lots of options out there. Ask for help when you need it!

2. Waiting until the last minute with schoolwork or studying for a test will only cause you more stress. Give yourself more time than you think you'll need.

3. If you have a learning disability, learn as much as you can about what may help you. And remember that you're smart, unique, and capable of amazing things.

4. When it comes to trying out for teams or activities, remember that persistence pays off. You may not get the role you want right away, but don't give up.

5. Figure out what sparks your interest when setting goals. Make your goals something meaningful to you.

6. When you set goals, write them down, along with the steps you need to get there. Make sure these are steps you can do and can finish in the near future.

7. If you're not getting along with one or more of your teachers, take the time to talk to them. Even though it may be intimidating, teachers are there to help you.

8. When starting a new school year, reach out to new people and new situations. This is your chance to try things you haven't tried before.

9. If someone is attacking you online, take a break from social media. Cyberbullying doesn't work without an audience.

10. Stand up for your friends when they are bullied, and ask them to help if a bully targets you.

GLOSSARY

advocate
To speak up for something.

AP (Advanced Placement)
Describing high school courses that offer college credit to those who pass an exam.

attention deficit hyperactivity disorder (ADHD)
A condition of the brain that affects a person's ability to focus and to control impulses.

bias
Prejudice in favor of or against one thing, person, or group compared with another, usually in a way considered to be unfair.

bisect
To divide into two parts.

confiscate
To take away or seize someone's property.

diagnose
To have symptoms classified as a disease or condition, usually by a medical professional.

dyslexia
A learning disability that affects the brain's ability to interpret written letters, numbers, and other symbols.

extracurricular
A student activity, such as a sport, that is connected with school but does not carry academic credit.

504 plan
A plan created by schools to accommodate students with physical or mental disabilities, protected by federal law.

incentive
A reward or prize to motivate and encourage you.

intervention
The act of stepping into a situation to prevent something from happening.

ISIS (Islamic State in Iraq and Syria)
An Islamist terrorist group.

procrastination
The act of intentionally putting off a task that needs to be done.

ADDITIONAL
RESOURCES

SELECTED BIBLIOGRAPHY

Homayoun, Ana. *The Myth of the Perfect Girl.* Perigee, 2013.

Karres, Erika V. Shearin, and Rebecca Branstetter. *The Conscious Parent's Guide to Raising Girls.* Adams Media, 2017.

Saltz, Gail. *The Power of Different: The Link Between Disorder and Genius.* Flatiron Books, 2017.

FURTHER READINGS

Amen, Daniel G. *Change Your Brain, Change Your Grades: The Secrets of Successful Students.* BenBella Books, 2019.

Baruch-Feldman, Caren. *The Grit Guide for Teens.* Instant Help, 2017.

Holsman, Jessica. *The High School Survival Guide: Your Roadmap to Studying, Socializing, and Succeeding.* Mango, 2016.

ONLINE RESOURCES

Booklinks
NONFICTION NETWORK
FREE! ONLINE NONFICTION RESOURCES

To learn more about surviving and thriving at school, please visit **abdobooklinks.com** or scan this QR code. These links are routinely monitored and updated to provide the most current information available.

For more information on this subject, contact or visit the following organizations:

College Board

250 Vesey St.
New York, NY 10281
collegeboard.org
866-630-9305

This nonprofit group administers the Advanced Placement courses and testing as well as the SAT college entrance tests.

Learning Disabilities Association of America

461 Cochran Rd., Suite 245
Pittsburgh, PA 15228
ldaamerica.org
412-341-1515

This organization provides support and resources to children and adults with learning disabilities.

StopBullying.gov

US Department of Health and Human Services
200 Independence Ave. SW
Washington, DC 20201
stopbullying.gov
877-696-6775

StopBullying.gov is run by the US Department of Health and Human Services. It provides ideas for prevention as well as resources for helping kids targeted by bullying.

INDEX

ABOUT THE
AUTHOR

SHANNON BERG

Shannon Berg is a young adult novelist, short story and nonfiction author, and poet. Shannon lives in Minnesota with her husband, two children, dog, and cat. Most of her spare time is spent working her way through the stack of books waiting to be read on her nightstand.